A Beginner's Guide to Becoming an Antiques Dealer

Antiques for Everyone

by
Christine Pym

Œ

Strategic Book Publishing and Rights Co.

Strategic Book Publishing and Rights Co.
12620 FM 1960, Suite A4-507
Houston, TX 77065
www.sbpra.com

ISBN: 978-1-62857-516-3

Design: Dedicated Book Services (www.netdbs.com)

Dedication

I wish to dedicate this book to the memory of my late dear father, Eric George Cowley (1927-2008), who was an upstanding local citizen and left his mark despite battling a long debilitating illness.

Acknowledgments

All photographs supplied courtesy of David J Pym Antiques (www.davidjpym.com).

Front cover imagery and artistic effects by Christopher Sadler and Abigail Pym, second year undergraduate students, photography, fashion and textiles.

Foreword

For the last twenty-five years, I have worked with a hands-on approach, from collecting and studying antiques and collectibles as a hobby all the way through to running a successful professional business. It seems appropriate to impart some of that knowledge of a very popular and fascinating profession to an increasingly inquisitive public.

Rene Lalique-'Suzanne'—c1925

Table of Contents

Introduction

The world of antiques is both fascinating and inexhaustible. England has a rich and colorful history which is probably one of the most envied in the world, and this heritage has afforded us a varied tapestry of antiques and collectibles. This includes pottery, pewter, and silver from the sixteenth and seventeenth centuries, early beautiful European porcelain from 1750 and coveted early Georgian furniture, up to a hugely productive nineteenth century Victorian period with fine antiques and collectibles of both a decorative and emotive, as well as an amusement nature.

The term "antique" is a loose description of items and artifacts made one hundred or more years ago and was in reference to early tax laws. Within the trade, the term also broadly encompasses the period prior to the end of World War II. Very few items were actually made during the war because many factories were requisitioned for the war effort, thereby causing them to cease production. Some prime factories, such as Meissen and Dresden in Germany, were significantly damaged or suffered socioeconomic depression. This created a void at the end of the Art Deco period that existed until the industry was able to find its feet. Eventually the Retro period, mainly influenced by America, took effect in the 1950s and 1960s.

Historic Periods

1. GEORGIAN AND REGENCY are periods of history normally defined as spanning the reigns of the first four Hanoverian kings of Great Britain (later the United Kingdom): George I, George II, George III, and George IV. The era covers the period from 1714 to 1830, incorporating the sub-period of the Regency defined by the regency of George IV as Prince of Wales during the illness of his father, George III.

The term "Georgian" is typically used in the contexts of social history, architecture and antiques. Antiques are also referred to as being from the "Regency" period. Georgian society and its preoccupations were well portrayed in the novels of writers such as Henry Fielding, Mary Shelley, and Jane Austen, characterized by the architecture of Robert Adam, John Nash, and James Wyatt and the emergence of the Gothic Revival style, which hearkened back to a supposed golden age of building design.

The flowering of the arts was most vividly shown in the emergence of the Romantic poets, principally through Samuel Taylor Coleridge, William Wordsworth, Percy Bysshe Shelley, William Blake, John Keats, Lord Byron and Robert Burns. Their work ushered in a new era of poetry, characterized by vivid and colourful language, evocative of elevating idea and themes.

The paintings of Thomas Gainsborough, Sir Joshua Reynolds and the young J.M.W. Turner and John Constable illustrated the changing world of the Georgian period—as did the work of designers like Capability Brown, the landscape designer.

It was a time of immense social change in Britain, with the beginnings of the Industrial Revolution, which began the process of intensifying class divisions, and the emergence of rival political parties like the Whigs and Tories.

In terms of antiques, it has left a wealth of stylized, romantic antiques such as silver, porcelain, furniture, and works of art, which today are highly regarded and can command large sums of money. However, many such antiques and works of art are preserved family heirlooms housed within surviving stately homes and country estates and infrequently reaching the open market. The passage of time has also contributed to the scarcity and rarity of such items that have survived in good condition.

Regency Clocks, dueling pistols, militaria and jewelry are examples of fine workmanship, and hence have become highly prized rare collectibles.

2. THE VICTORIAN ERA of British history was the period of Queen Victoria's reign from 20 June 1837 until her death on 22 January 1901. Culturally, there was a transition away from the rationalism of the Georgian period and towards romanticism and mysticism with regard to religion, social values, and the arts.

In 1851, the Great Exhibition, the first World Fair, showcased the latest innovations. At its centre was Crystal Palace, a modular glass and iron structure.

"Victorian decorative arts" is a term that refers to the style of decorative arts during the Victorian era. Victorian design is widely viewed as having indulged in a grand excess of ornament, and the era is known for its interpretation and eclectic revival of historic styles mixed with the introduction of Middle Eastern and Asian influences in furniture, fittings, and interior decoration. The arts and crafts movement, the aesthetic movement, Anglo-Japanese style, and Art Nouveau have their beginnings in the late Victorian era.

Wallpaper was often made in elaborate floral patterns with primary colors (red, blue, and yellow) in the backgrounds and overprinted with colors of cream and tan. This was followed by Gothic art-inspired papers in earth tones with stylized leaf and floral patterns. William Morris was one of the most influential designers of wallpaper and fabrics during the latter half of the Victorian period. Morris was inspired to use Medieval and Gothic tapestries in his work.

From the 1850's interiors became very bourgeois with heavy curtains showing a desire for privacy. Funeral customs were marked by photographic records. Queen Victoria's own private mourning of Prince Albert reflected the somber mood by the use of black stoneware and porcelain and dark jewelry.

Natural history became increasingly an "amateur's" activity. Particularly in Britain and the United States, this grew into hobbies such as the study of birds, butterflies, seashells, beetles, and wild flowers, all of which are recorded influences in art designs on porcelain and pottery.

3. ART NOUVEAU is a French term meaning "new art," also known as Jugendstil, a German word meaning "youth style," and it covers the period from 1890 to 1910. It was most popular in Europe, but its eventual influence was global. It could be said that Art Nouveau was the first twentieth century modern style, and it was the first style to stop looking backwards in history for ideas, taking inspiration instead from what it saw around it, in particular, the natural world. Its style is depicted by the following:

- sinuous, elongated curvy lines
- the whiplash line
- vertical lines and height
- stylized flowers, leaves, roots, buds and seed pods
- the female form—in a pre-Raphaelite pose with long, flowing hair
- exotic woods, marquetry, iridescent glass, silver and semi-precious stones

Influences of the Art Nouveau period include:

- arts and crafts—Art Nouveau shared the same belief in good quality and fine craftsmanship, but was happy with mass production.
- Rococo style
- botanical research

Important names associated with the Art Nouveau period include:

- Charles René MacKintosh—architect and designer of furniture and jewelry
- Alphonse Mucha—posters
- Aubrey Beardsley—book illustrations

Lorenzyl Cold Painted Bronze—c1930

- Louis Comfort Tiffany—lighting
- René Lalique—glass and jewelry
- Emile Galle—ceramics, glass and furniture
- Victor Horta—architect
- WMF—stylized "lady figure" and arts and craft—silver-plated pewter tableware
- Moorcroft—pottery

This was a highly influential and stylized period which has become one of the most iconic and highly-collected. Due to mass production, many Art Nouveau pieces are not valuable, although they are still highly desirable. If the item is made by a famous and accredited designer, however, the price soars (see later section on Fine Antiques).

4. ART DECO (circa 1908 to 1935) began in Europe, particularly the city of Paris, in the early years of the twentieth century. It didn't really take hold until after World War I, and it reigned until the outbreak of World War II. This time, the style was depicted by the following:

- geometric and angular shapes
- chrome, glass, shiny fabrics
- mirrors and mirror tiles
- stylized images of airplanes, cars, cruise liners and skyscrapers
- nature motifs—shells, sunrises, flowers and furs

Influences of the Art Deco period include:

- Art Nouveau—keeping the nature motifs of its predecessor, it discarded its flowing, organic shape and pastels for bolder materials and colours, such as chrome and black.
- Cubism—painters like Picasso were experimenting with space, angles, and geometry.
- Early Hollywood—the glamorous world of the silver screen filtered through to design, which used shiny fabrics, subdued lighting, and mirrors.
- Cocktail cabinets and smoking paraphernalia became highly-fashionable.

Important names associated with the Art Deco period include:

- Eileen Gray—furniture
- Raymond Templier—jewelry
- Clarice Cliff—china

Goldscheider Wall Mask—c1930

- René Lalique—glass and jewelry
- Moorcroft—pottery

Other influences on the period include:

- 1912—RMS Titanic sank
- 1922—Tomb of Egyptian pharaoh Tutankhamen discovered
- 1922—The book "Ulysses" by James Joyce published
- 1931—Empire State Building completed

Film stars of the Art Deco period included:

- Greta Garbo
- Marlene Dietrich
- Fred Astaire
- Ginger Rogers

In addition to all these influences, the Charleston and the tango were the latest dance crazes, jazz was born, and singer Josephine Baker thrilled audiences in Paris.

5. RETRO PERIOD—A culturally outdated or aged style, trend, mode or fashion from the overall post-modern past that has since that time become functionally or superficially the norm once again. The use of "Retro" style iconography and imagery can be interjected into post-modern art, advertising, mass media, and etcetera. It generally implies a vintage of at least fifteen or twenty years.

In terms of the antiques trade, the 1940's and 1950's, in particular, began mainly in the United States, where rock artists like Buddy Holly and Elvis Presley greatly influenced the music world and fashion. Popular items included leather handbags, "bell-bottom" jeans, big sunglasses, fedoras, funk jackets (commonly called Adidas classics) and shoes, small neckties, chiffon scarves, sports equipment, and skinny jeans. Makeup from the Retro period is distinguished by heavily-lined eyes and bright red lipstick, hairstyles that included pompadours, ponytails, and ducktails, in addition to other styles that modeled film stars of the 1940's and 1950's.

This continued into the 1960's and 1970's, where rock influences, particularly from Britain, included Led Zeppelin, Black Sabbath, Jimi Hendrix, the Beatles and Pink Floyd. Fashion, too, became iconic—with psychedelic genre shapes and bold colours. A popular designer of the period was Mary Quant.

In the 1970's, Biba and Laura Ashley became popular for their retro and vintage fashion. They are still designing today.

Rare WMF Desk Ink Stand—c1920

Chapter 1

Starting Points

ONE WELL KNOWN SUCCESSFUL antiques dealer when asked to describe the secret of success said, "To have for sale a pot of gold at a next to nothing price." In other words, it is important to have quality or valuable items at the cheapest possible price.

The most important feature of an antique or of a collector's item is its uniqueness, a combination of the fact that the item was made at a time when labour and man hours were at a premium and, nine times out of ten, those skills could not be replicated today for the same price. The fact, too, that the item cannot be found in the High Street shops would make it immediately more desirable.

One of the most important attributes of being an antiques dealer is having an "eye" or a keen awareness of artistic taste, fine detail, and value. A person is most likely born with an artistic eye, however, having a keen interest in a specialist area—such as a collector's hobby—coupled with the knowledge gained from intense study about the chosen subject, is the most frequent entry point. Marketing and industry knowledge can be gained through experience and a hands-on approach of trial and error.

The dealer may also possess special areas of knowledge or expertise that has come from previous employment in the fields of, engineering, electronics, horology, carpentry or restoration. Any of these skills could be used on their own to develop a specific area of expertise or hobby to supplement and assist an established dealer or retailer.

Other abilities, such as marketing, presentation, and sales may have been gained from working in a retail business or other employment, in addition to general life skills. Sometimes a dealer begins with a hobby or interest that is separate from full-time employment. It is an individual preference how much time a person wants to devote to it.

One of the most appealing characteristics of the antiques business is its scope, the endless variances of each item which gives them each their own unique history, and the fact that hitherto unknown items are constantly being discovered. There are no precise benchmarks. The value of an item is dictated by the current market. This makes the antiques business particularly exciting, but on the other hand, there is a long learning curve which is quite possibly indefinite. Also, the business is transitory and subject to fashions, trends, and economic fluctuations.

Chapter 2

Specialist Areas

SOME OF THE BEST ways to decide your specialist area, if you have not already done so, are to visit auction rooms to see the types of items for sale in the raw, or antique fairs where particular collections are showcased by individual dealers, or antique arcades which encompass a wide range of different articles of every description. Ultimately, antiques shops or specialist retail units will show items in their best, possibly restored condition, and expertly presented.

In choosing a specialist area, be guided by things you are most comfortable with and that hold a particular interest for you. Most dealers' collections have been obtained over a long period of time by careful and painstaking selection and research. In addition to the work, a great deal of pleasure will have been experienced in searching for pieces, and owning them, and it is safe to say that the charm of antiques/collectibles is that it would be impossible for anyone, no matter how experienced or knowledgeable, to be considered an "absolute" expert. There is always something new to learn, and that is part of the fun of it.

The antiques world is constantly changing worldwide and is governed by what is in fashion as well as the economic climate. Having said that, an item which, at its inception, was an item of quality and skilled manufacture and/or intrinsic artistic value, will predominantly retain that mark of quality and desirability throughout its existence. This, in turn, will be reflected in its open market price.

New discoveries are made all the time, where an item has lain in a private collection and nothing like it has been

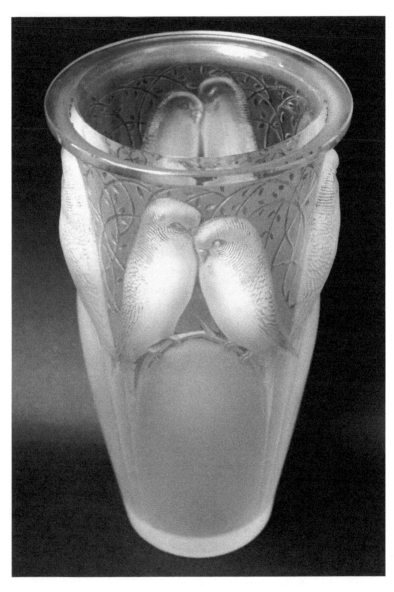

Rene Lalique 'Ceylan' opal/blue—c1924

seen before—or its worth or desirability is undervalued by an owner who may have inherited it—and it subsequently comes up for sale possibly at a boot fair or house clearance auction. Over the passage of time, many different styles and types of artifacts have been created, and it would be impossible to account for every single item.

How often it is that someone says, "If only I had kept so-and-so item. Look how much it is worth now." That is precisely the nature of antiques, that no-one could possibly predict for sure what will be a valuable item or collectible in the future. Not even René Lalique or William Moorcroft knew how desirable their products would be during their lifetimes. A savvy dealer or collector may use his knowledge and expertise to choose those articles which he thinks might possess the "x factor" and thereby make himself a pot of gold. A buyer, too, might purchase an undervalued item simply because he/she likes it and wants to enjoy it in his/her home or otherwise. It could be utilitarian artifact, which is particularly well made or unique and better quality than anything similar of modern manufacture. Some items are already accredited, making them items to look out for (see Fine Antiques Section). Such is the mystery and excitement of antiques.

The condition of an antique or collectible is all important, and although "old stapled repairs" on pieces of porcelain and china denote character, the most desired condition to command the best price will be as near to its original state as possible.

Chapter 3

Reproductions and Fakes

IT IS IMPORTANT TO note that an item whose condition is "too perfect" will immediately arouse suspicion as to whether it is a reproduction or fake. It is only through knowledge and research that a dealer would be able to test its authenticity. As a general rule of thumb, if the seller is unsure of an item's originality and age, don't make any assertions or assumptions, which could be construed as misleading statements or- in the worse case scenario—a trade description misrepresentation that could even result in legal action.

Throughout history, very clever, painstaking reproductions have been made. For example, some nineteenth century pieces of furniture are actually reproductions of styles made one hundred years earlier; also, pieces may have been changed or been modified, either of which will have a bearing on the price. This is why dealing in antiques is exhaustive and fascinating, but ultimately it can, in the case of "fine antiques"—those which have a proven track record or pedigree—be a substantive investment. The arts and antiques investment market is considered to be of a more speculative nature, however large sums of money can be realized even over short periods of time if the investment is wise and considered.

That is why it is extremely important that any item purchased for resale should be thoroughly researched in order that correct information is available to a prospective buyer. This criteria is unique to the antiques industry, as other retail establishments will source their products directly from factories or warehouses, where precise origins of their merchandise is known, and it may in fact have been manufactured as recently as yesterday. One of the most compelling qualities of antiques or collectibles is that they are items which are unlikely to be found in the High Street shops. It is that quality which must be qualified and clarified, as there is nothing more infuriating to a purchaser than to later discover that his treasured "antique" is in fact a modern fake.

It is considered good practice within the industry to obtain a full detailed written receipt on headed paper at the point of purchase. This is certainly the case for "fine antiques" as it will authenticate the sale and provide details for future contact and insurance purposes. From the dealer's perspective, he will also need to retain copies of all purchases and sales in order to correlate his books for tax purposes (for discussion in a later section).

An antique business proprietor, in common with all other retail establishment and business owners, will enhance the success and longevity of his business by operating in a professional and trustworthy manner. This will help to build long-term relationships.

Chapter 4

Buy Antiques

AUCTION ROOMS ARE CONSTANTLY an area of mystery and intrigue. They are not new, many dating back several hundreds of years, and they are an excellent means of selling and buying unwanted and/or valuable items.

Their apparent mystery lies in the inherent "risk" of making any gesture which might be construed as a "bid" at an inopportune and unintentional point in the auction's proceedings. Once a bid has been successful, the law requires the bidder to pay for the item, together with the published charges of the auction room.

This is not as precarious as it may seem because a bidder is registered before the start of the auction, and his/her allocated bid number (paddle) is required to validate any purchase of any lot during the sale. The greatest actual risk is that a bidder may become carried away within the auction process and ends up paying well in excess of his intended budget—or alternatively, he fails to note that there is as much as a twenty-five percent charge added on top of the hammer price.

The general rules for attending an auction would be to:

+ View the auction well beforehand, and in particular any item(s) which you may consider purchasing, to take account of condition, repairs, construction and other factors—thus heeding the warning phrase "Buyer beware."
+ Decide your ceiling price for the item, and don't get caught up in the flow so that you overspend.

- Note the "Buyers Premium"—i.e. the percentage charge detailed in the Catalogue Rules, which are payable on top of the hammer price.

The attraction of the auction is the possibility of acquiring a desired item at a below market average price. This may occur if there is insufficient interest at the auction from buyers in attendance, or the item may be undervalued in one area of the country in relation to another. Nowadays most auction rooms publish online catalogues, and any fine antiques or collectors' items will most likely be spotted and bids could even be made online or by telephone worldwide. But it is still the "luck of the draw" that creates the excitement and anticipation to be felt at the event. Most people feel the "buzz" and anticipation just as the auction is about to begin, especially in the case of a specialist event.

Antique dealers and traders that have their own specialist trading areas will be aware of their own market prices and what they would consider a good price for an item. Some dealers may be more established with better retail outlets or have a customer or other dealer, in the case of a runner, already envisaged to "move the item on." The different trading variations are endless.

It is also possible to sell private items at auction. Once again, the seller should be aware of the "premium" which would be deducted from the hammer price. It can vary, and in some instances may make it more advantageous to approach a dealer directly.

Antique fairs and open air markets have become well established across the country and will be advertised locally in dedicated antique publications, in the local press, or online. The advantage of visiting these is that they are trade fairs and one fair venue will encompass many different stands, from dealers throughout the country and in many specialist areas, ranging from lower priced items through to fine antiques.

Antique arcades and centres are similar to antique fairs in that they offer different individually operated retail units where separate dealers pay a rent to display their own particular range of artifacts and a buyer may then often deal directly with the dealer to negotiate the best price. Unlike antique fairs, which are most likely held once a month or quarterly throughout the year at different venues, the centres are permanent retail outlets or small integral shops in a town where a person may browse at his leisure and the range of antiques is constantly changing.

Shops are an extension of the arcade centre concept, in that one proprietor will now professionally own and operate his own retail outlet with usually increased floor space and full control of the premises. Quite often they house specialist collections and fine antiques. That is not to say, however, that some antique centres may not also offer a range of fine antiques, dependant on the setup, including levels of security and amenities.

Boot fairs to a certain extent, are pro formas of open air antique markets, except that their merchandise also includes general household items together with collectors' items and some antiques fresh to the market. They became very popular in the 1980's, as an extension of jumble sales and table top sales. They are a means for any private individual to directly present his unwanted household items for sale on a casual basis, and later in this book, they will also be discussed as a possible good first starter retail outlet.

A first good test, similar to the concept adopted by some of the current popular antiques television programmes, is to allow yourself a conservative budget of, say just five pounds, to search among the different stalls and see what you can buy for your money. Some items will probably be priced at a few pence or pounds. Remember to look for items of interest that you think you would be able to resell for a profit, including those items which require some restoration processes, within your own capabilities.

Quite often, a household will have accrued and inherited antique and collectors' items and other bric-a-brac over many decades, and this outlet has the advantage of being able to sell those items without paying auction fees or searching out other sales areas, as they attract dealers and collectors as well as the general public.

An antiques runner is a person in the business who may or may not front his own retail outlet. He operates by sourcing antiques and collectors' items to resell to other known retail outlets and dealers. He uses his extensive knowledge and expertise to comb buyers' sites in search of suitable items to then resell to his contacts. They are an invaluable aid to established dealers who do not always have time to put in the legwork themselves, and this forms unique powerful partnerships and networks within the trade. Dealers may also cross-refer prospective customers to trade contacts and other dealers.

Art Deco W. Lange 'Fencer'-cold-painted bronze—c1930

Chapter 5

Restoration

WHEN RESTORING AN OBJECT—for example, a piece of furniture—it is important to research the item thoroughly beforehand, depending on the value of the item. If it is a rustic piece, then a thorough cleaning with solvent or just soapy water will initially suffice to remove surface grime. Then a suitable antique wax may be applied, dependant on the type of wood.

Other types of furniture may require repairs, for example loose or missing door hinges, door knobs, or handles; and it would be important to try to match existing screws and other period features when doing these repairs. Repair of veneers and inlays are much more specialized and require more skill.

If the item has significant value, it may be better to approach a reputable cabinet maker or restorer to effect the repair(s), as a botched attempt at a repair could result in the item's value being lessened or even completely destroyed.

Some antiques may be sold "as found," which is when a buyer purchases the object in a condition that is identified as "unrestored," or in the case of porcelain and pottery, damaged or cracked. He may then undertake to have the item restored himself or to simply accept the identified "flaw."

In cases of unique rarity, and in such an instance it becomes the only way to own an item, the inherent damage and condition will not inhibit its value and salability. In fact, it would be preferable that the item remain unrestored. In other instances, where it is evident the item has been repaired, a dealer should make reference to that fact in a written description, because in the case of items of that have significant value; it can quite dramatically affect the price. There are some extremely gifted and skilled glass and porcelain/pottery repairers who may have already been employed to restore an item to such a high standard that it will be impossible to detect with the naked eye. An experienced dealer will have conducted a "blue or black light" and other industry tests to decipher originality, which he would then disclose to a prospective buyer. Failure to disclose such facts may be construed as deception.

Once again, research and professional advice are the keys to good practice in handling valuable heritage artifacts.

Silver, brass, and copper require the correct industrial cleaners, and it is important not to over-clean them, as this may reduce an item's value, or damage it entirely in the case of silver plate. In some cases, the plating may already have been removed to such a degree that it has destroyed its intrinsic value and beauty, thereby leaving the item virtually worthless.

Silver plating has been carried out for hundreds of years, quite often with copper as the conductive base metal. The silver, in leaf form, would be rolled over the copper by hand, which is a complex, skilled procedure. Significantly, when the plating wears off and the copper beneath is exposed, it is referred to in the business as "bleed." Such items, if professionally re-plated, should have the same roll-over silver leaf process applied, but the temptation may be, due to its expense, to electroplate or dip the item. This is a more modern technique first adopted commercially in the 1850's by Elkingtons. Patents for commercial electroplating of nickel, brass, tin, and zinc meant large scale electroplating baths, and equipment could be used to plate numerous larger objects. Also in the late nineteenth century, the advent and development of electric generators with higher currents also helped the process. Items thus plated carry the "EPNS" stamp for "Electroplated Nickel Silver" or less commonly, "EPBM" for "Electroplated Britannia Metal" object.

In the case of electric lamps, these should be professionally rewired and earthed. Care should be taken to ensure that plugs are removed from electrical items or, alternatively, that they have been readapted to meet current British Standards.

Some industry professionals may enter the antiques industry in a support role, initially offering invaluable services as a hobby, which may later lead to a professional business. A top antiques dealer will often possess a wide range of professional skills and qualifications including woodwork, engineering, and electronics. Computer skills, marketing, and retail experience may also be extremely beneficial.

Chapter 6

Retailing

HAVING CONDUCTED YOUR RESEARCH, now it's time to get started and to test your retail capabilities. Good starting places are car boot fairs. As already mentioned, boot fairs provide an excellent low pressure first opportunity for a private person to take part, either as a buyer or seller, in one of the many different regular outlets held throughout the country.

In the same way that items can be purchased for a few pence or pounds, for a nominal cost, a seller may set up his or her table to display wares including direct household items, bric-a-brac, and some newly-acquired antiques. He or she is then in the vicinity to both buy and sell and to negotiate "deals."

This is a good place to experience the thrill of meeting and engaging with the public, to learn how well your things sell and to gauge which of your chosen objects sell best. From here, you will start to gain experience and begin to determine whether or not you are cut out for the industry.

Once you have acquired experience, together with a suitable collection of antiques, memorabilia, or collectibles, you may feel confident enough to progress to hiring a "stand" at a local antiques fair or open air market. The objective here will be to cover your daily rental outlay and travel costs as well as returning an overall profit.

In these ways, the process of buying and selling is repeated as you reinvest profits back into the business in order to acquire and expand your stock. Ultimately, you will have a sufficient collection to consider renting a retail unit in an antiques centre or other establishment. Once you take this step, you will need to be aware of notice periods and regulations being imposed by the owner(s) of such premises, as some form of binding business contract will be operational.

Remember, too, that as you commit to paying rents, you will need to make a profit, and in turn, repeat the circle of sourcing and replenishing your stock. At this point, only time will tell whether you are cut out for the job!

You will also have entered the retail business where fair trading rules and regulations will apply, as well as statutory tax obligations.

Chapter 7

Statutory Regulations

AN ANTIQUE BUSINESS IS in essence a retail business and follows the same rules and regulations, which include the following:

The business must be registered for tax purposes and books must be kept recording purchases, sales, and profits. Even if after the first year no profit has been made—or after taking into account a personal allowance and other allowable expenses such as travel and rents, a loss is recorded—that loss is accountable for tax purposes and can then be offset against successive years.

As the business proves successful, and if the profits exceed the current stated VAT (Value Added Tax) threshold allowance pro rata for any three consecutive months (currently in the region of seventy-five thousand pounds annual turnover), then VAT at the stipulated rate (currently twenty percent of the full item's value) must also be paid on top of standard income tax. Within the antiques industry, VAT is not added separately on top of the agreed retail price, as in the case of new items or services, but is paid entirely out of profits. The industry is not separately regulated and each individual business is accountable for its own professional conduct. Trading Standards and Fair Trading Rules apply in the same way as any high street retail business, and therefore should be referenced and observed.

The owner of a professional business, in order to succeed in the long run, must inspire trust and deliver satisfaction in all business dealings. Longevity is established through the owner's hard work and continued attention to business.

Art Deco 'Seal' Lamp—c1930

Chapter 8

Online Auction Websites

ONLINE AUCTION WEBSITES, SUCH as EBay, are one of the most recent additions to the antique dealer's options for buying and selling. An individual account is set up, and for a nominal listing fee items ranging from a few pence to thousands of pounds may be advertised for sale or purchased online. A percentage fee (usually around ten percent of the item's value) is only applied if a sale is secured.

There are options to "Buy It Now," which effectively is the seller's preferred retail price, or "Buy It Now or Make an Offer," which is self-explanatory. If none of these preset options are deployed, the item continues to auction within a designated time-frame starting at an agreed price which may be as low as a few pence or pounds.

The main advantage of using this type of system is that there is quite often worldwide coverage. There are no monthly stall rentals or overheads and transactions can be conducted from a home base.

It is important to mount good quality photographs to accompany the listing, especially in the case of fine antiques where different views of important vantage points will encourage quality sales.

Rene Lalique 'Camargue' Sepia Vase—c1942

The website provider will exercise control over trade principles. If, for example, a subscriber is reported to be unreliable or dishonest, his membership is revoked and he will be barred from the website. Also the individual performance ratings, (which are based on customers' input about experiences they have had with the seller) provide a reference for prospective new business.

Details such as the cost of postage and packaging are included on the website and negotiated and settled between the seller and buyer within the terms of sale. Payments made using Pay pal are regulated and secure.

One of the main drawbacks of using the online auction website is that item(s) cannot be viewed in the flesh. If the seller's descriptions, photographs and ratings are honest and professional, however, a trusting relationship may be formed over a period of time between buyer and seller which will be to both of their benefit. Alternatively, specific details may be discussed by telephone and/or viewing appointments arranged prior to purchase.

In the case of established traders, there are often links provided to a separate business website that supplies information and reassurance of the seller's trade credentials, and further fruitful business liaisons may be formed.

This trading method can never override a buyer's preference to browse and view a full range of items within retail premises with the possibility of obtaining first-hand information and discourse with the seller.

Chapter 9

Fine Antiques

FINE ANTIQUES ARE THOSE items that already have a proven track record and price strategy, i.e.: they have, over the passage of time, accrued a value.

Examples of such items are Lalique, Moorcroft, WMF (Wurttembergische Metallwarenfabrik), Clarice Cliff, Worcester porcelain, silver, militaria, Long Case clocks, various furniture, Art Deco lamps, art, fine jewelry and watches and other intrinsic specialist and rare collectors' items.

The value of fine antiques is depicted mainly by their desirability, rarity, quality and timeless beauty. They also cannot be reproduced; they represent a historic period or mood, and are, quite often a tangible piece of history.

To use a case in point, **dueling pistols** are an example of such fine antiques. They represent a bizarre historical period, dating from about 1730 to 1850 (specifically 1780 to 1810) when private disputes and matters of honour were settled by duel.

Numerous accounts tell of "pistols at dawn" or "pistols at ten paces," when two members of the landed gentry or even politicians would meet at an agreed location to duel with pistols, accompanied by their "seconds." An agreed distance was set between the two adversaries, quite often it was ten paces. If the assailant had not fired after three seconds, the challenger would have the opportunity of a direct shot. There were quite often fatalities.

In some American states during the mid-1850's as many as fourteen duels a week were fought, although in England sensibilities against the feuds had grown to such an extent that Queen Victoria ruled it illegal when she came to the throne in 1837, and the practice had virtually disappeared by 1850.

European and English pistols were considered to be the finest, although not the most highly decorated. One of the earliest names associated with dueling pistols was that of John Twigg, who is known for the introduction of boxed pistols. All the necessary parts to load the weapons were included with the pistols in a convenient sized box that could be carried easily under one arm. Makers Robert Wogdon closely followed in the trade in 1785, and after that John Manton. Other makers were also commissioned, due to the demand for personal defense in the early 1800's.

Nowadays a cased set of pistols by any of these makers can reach forty thousand pounds or more and are highly collected. Many reside in private collections or museums as "works of astonishing craftsmanship and precision."

Such was the heightened demand for precision and attention to detail, that it would take gunsmiths about six months to make a cased set of dueling pistols. Already seasoned, worn horse nails or wagon wheel nails were collected and hammered down for use in the barrels in order to give them sufficient strength. Also great detail was paid to the figuring and shaping of the wood and the individual refinements by skilled workmen and apprentices, which added to the length of time it took to complete a boxed set. They are highly coveted today and remain tangible and awesome evidence of the idiosyncrasies of a bygone age.

Before leaving the subject of weaponry, it should be noted that subsequent forms of weapons and ammunition are also avidly collected. Bullets that were later used in rifles and guns for the cowboys of the Wild West, including Colts, revolvers, and Army and Navy standards are also very popular. The array of antique militaria, including complete sets of armour, is a tangible record of this country's colourful history, both in war and peace.

Another maker of fine antiques is renowned jewelry maker **René Joules Lalique** (6 April 1860 to 5 May 1945).

He was born in Ay, France, and spent his early life learning the methods of design and art. In 1872, when he was twelve, he attended the College Turgot where he started drawing and sketching. After the death of his father two years later, Lalique began working as an apprentice to goldsmith Louis Aucoc in Paris and attended evening classes at the École des Arts Decoratifs. He worked there from 1874 to 1876 and subsequently spent two years at the Crystal Palace School of Art, in Sydenham, London.

At the Sydenham Art College, his skills for graphic design were improved, and he further developed a naturalistic approach to art. When he returned to England, he worked as a freelance artist, designing pieces of jewelry for French jewelers Cartier, Boucheron, and others. In 1885, René Lalique opened his own business and designed and began to make his own jewelry and other glass pieces.

By 1890, Lalique was recognized as one of France's foremost Art Nouveau jewelry designers, creating innovative pieces for Samuel Bing's new Paris shop, Maison de l'Art Nouveau. He went on to become one of the most famous in his field, his name being synonymous with creativity, beauty, and quality.

In the 1920's, he became noted for his work in the Art Deco style. He was responsible for the walls of lighted glass and elegant coloured glass columns which filled the dining room and "grand salon" of the SS Normandie and the interior fittings, cross, screens, rereads, and font of St. Matthew's Church at Millbrook in Jersey (Lalique's Glass Church). His earlier experiences in Ay were his defining influence in his later work. As a result, many of his jewelry pieces and vases showcase plants, insects, flowers, and flowing lines.

Lalique glass has proved to be one of the most coveted and enduring antiques, with some of his early pieces commanding huge prices at auction; and for this reason, it is highly sought after and collected, not only for its beauty but also as an investment. Some of the original moulds have survived and are being used by the factory in Wingen-sur-Moder to regenerate modern versions. The opalescent techniques, however, are usually absent from such pieces because these were intensive, complicated, technical and artistic procedures whose chemical makeup and artistry was not passed down through the generations.

Lalique's son, Mark, who took over the factory in 1945 when Lalique died, employed his own artistic influences and ideas, which included the introduction of lead crystal instead of glass and changed the look and value of the pieces. Upon Mark's death in 1977, René's granddaughter, Marie Claude-Lalique (1936-2003), who was also a glass maker, introduced some famous frosting techniques until her death in Fort Myers, Florida.

It is important to obtain a full written appraisal and bonafide receipt from an accredited dealer when purchasing fine antiques of this nature in order to be assured of an item's authenticity and originality.

William Moorcroft (1872-1945) was born in Burslem, Staffordshire. He studied art at Burslem, then in London and Paris. He experimented with his own pottery designs around 1896, while working for James Macintyre & Co., Ltd, the latter being well known for its expert tube-liners and decorators.

He first produced Aurelian Ware, which was partly decorated with transfers and partly painted by hand. He developed highly lustred glazes and used oriental shapes and decorations. Some of his techniques were closely-guarded trade secrets.

Moorcroft then developed his famous Florian Ware during the early 1900's Art Nouveau period, using heavy slip and a translucent glaze which produces brilliance of colour. Much of the output was sold through Liberty & Co., in London and Tiffany, in New York.

William Moorcroft set up his own factory at Cobridge in 1913 with staff from Macintryes. His work was known for quality design and decoration, and in 1928 Queen Mary made him "Potter to the Queen," which was stamped on the pottery. William's son, Walter, took over the pottery in

Moorcroft 'Florian' Vase—c1901

1945 just before William's death and the pottery received its second royal appointment a year later, in 1946.

Moorcroft pottery is still produced today, utilizing the same original techniques, at the Burslem Factory and has an active collector's club following.

The pottery in general has achieved fine art recognition, with many early designs realizing values of three and four figures. The reputation and recognition of quality has remained to this day, and there are no direct replicas or fakes—although other potters, including Doulton have produced their own versions of Flambes.

A Flambe description is applied when the original pot has been re-fired at an extremely high temperature to achieve red and brown hues on top of the existing colours, resulting in a totally original colouration. Needless to say, many pots were lost in this process because they shattered under the extreme heat. Also, as the effects were incalculable and indeterminate, there was no guarantee that the finished result would be artistically acceptable. Those which have deemed artistic acceptance and beauty generally carry a higher price tag and are exquisite.

The design which probably most encompasses the Moorcroft image is the "Pomegranate" design which predominately has a dark blue background with mellow reds and greens. This design spans approximately twenty years of production between the 1920's and 1940's, and for this reason has become synonymous with Moorcroft's dark rich colour tones.

There are many other very rare and collectible designs. Of course, only a limited quantity has survived the years intact, and it is only with retrospect that we are able to compare and chose the most perfect and pleasingly artistic pieces, which is a common trait with all other antiques.

WMF (Wurttembergische Metallwarenfabrik), which translates into English as "Metalware factory of Wurttemberg," is a tableware manufacturer founded in 1853 in Geislingen an der Steige, Germany, by the miller Daniel Straub and the

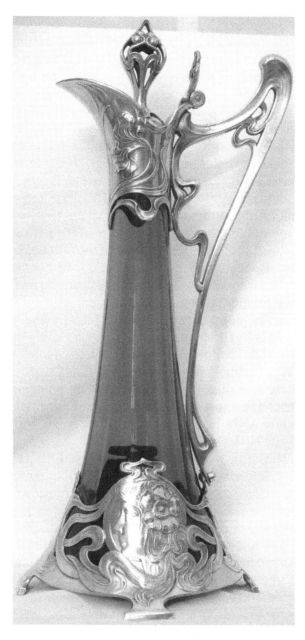

WMF Green 'Lady Head' Wine Jug—c1905

brothers Schweizer. The factory was originally opened as a metal repairing workshop. Around 1900, they were the world's largest producer and exporter of household metal ware, mainly in the Jugendstil, or Art Nouveau style. They are best known for the period of Albert Mayer, sculptor and designer, who was director of the WMF Art Studio from 1884 to 1914.

In 1905, WMF produced a catalogue of silver-plated pewter tableware with stylised lady figures and art nouveau designs, and it is this range which has become the most coveted and collected in the antiques world as synonymous of Art Nouveau. WMF pieces are particularly regarded for their quality and attention to detail when compared with other manufacturers of similar artifacts of the period.

In the illustration, you can see one of the rare and beautiful quality items, currently still available, which have survived in near pristine condition. The exquisite detailing and artistry has proved timeless and highly desirable.

It should be pointed out that quality and authenticity of these pieces are of great importance in determining the value, as an item that has lost its original plating, patina, original glass insert, or liner may also have suffered other damage. In this case the value will have decreased so significantly as to make it almost worthless on the open market. The items should never be cleaned or polished to the point that it damages the silver plating.

Jewelry retailing is a huge subject in itself. Experience is required to source quality items, whether they are genuine antiques, retro or modern vintage styles, at the correct price and to develop a niche market.

Once again, in order to run a successful business, it will be necessary to establish a reputation for being professional, dealing in quality and with impeccable ethics, during several years of trading. This will also include keeping records of repairing, modifying, and sizing (in the case of rings) in addition to backup from a properly-qualified jeweler and attention to detail. From a buyer's perspective, there are universally acknowledged benchmark standards to help decide value for money:

The Four C's:

- Colour
- Carat
- Clarity, and
- Cut

. . . And when buying a vintage ring, possibly two more:

- Condition, and
- Character

On the whole, the richer the colour of the stone the more valuable, but this is very much a matter of personal taste, and the most important factor is how much you like it. Sometimes paler or darker colours can be more appealing.

The carat is the weight or size of the stone, which is the main factor in its price, especially in the case of diamonds. The "rough" would need to be of sufficient gem-stone quality and will dictate the maximum carat size achievable in each individual circumstance. It will then entail a lapidary's skill to cut the stone in the best way to obtain and display an individual stone's own unique beauty and natural sparkle.

The clarity can vary. Marks within the stone are known as "inclusions" and can detract greatly from the appearance of the ring—and therefore its value—although some inclusions can add character to a stone.

Some gemstones, such as emeralds, are known for "le jardin" inclusions, which are intrinsic to its makeup, and rubies are rare without at least a few "fine silks". In fact, a jeweler's first inspection under magnification will often be to ascertain whether or not it is a genuine gem. Indeed, in Georgian and Victorian times many paste and synthetics were cleverly made to replicate natural gemstones, as it was very difficult to mine and cut the genuine article. Such jewelry was so intrinsically and exquisitely made that very often it doesn't affect their value.

Condition is important in vintage jewelry, and it is necessary when buying to check claws and signs of wear to determine if repair is necessary. Character is what sets vintage rings apart, as the same quality of craftsmanship in a modern ring is almost impossible to find and would be outrageously expensive. Rings of vintage beauty and quality are simply not made any more, except perhaps for the very rich. Generally speaking, vintage rings are generally less expensive than their modern counterparts and offer better value for the money.

Speaking again to integrity, it is imperative to apply the correct descriptions to any items you have for sale, together with disclosing any known damage or imperfections in the pieces.

In common with other antiques, many factors affect the value of jewelry, as well as the aforementioned criteria. For example, current fashions and popularity, as well as the rarity of a piece will affect its value. The market price of precious metals such as platinum, gold, and silver are also relevant in terms of weight content, which is measured in grams, in determining an item's value.

Platinum, which literally translated from the Spanish term *platina*, means "little silver." It is a dense, malleable, ductile, precious gray-white transition metal, and it is currently the most expensive natural white metal used for making fine jewelry. This is because only a few hundred tonnes are produced annually due to its scarcity. Its resistance to wear and tarnish, as well as its malleability, made it particularly popular in the early 1900's. Prior to that, silver had been used, as it had a lower melting point.

White gold has become increasingly popular. It is an alloy of gold with at least one white metal added, normally nickel, manganese, or palladium. The different properties of each alloy will be deployed in the piece, depending on the required purpose, i.e.: setting gemstones, or the requisite durability of an item.

The carat description will depict the purity of the base gold with an added whitish hue. Such gold is also often rhodium plated to improve the white colour and brightness.

Gold still remains the most malleable natural precious metal. Its market value will fluctuate marginally, along with diamonds and other precious gemstones.

Chapter 10

Conclusion

THE ANTIQUES WORLD IS extensive and inexhaustible. It would be impossible to describe every subject in detail. A plethora of detailed reference books exists on every conceivable aspect of buying and selling antiques, and quite often they can be found on the second-hand market. Also, the Internet provides vast references on the subject.

This book is a general introduction to some of the most popular areas of the antique business and is intended to help anyone wishing to enter this fascinating industry.

Chapter 11

Top Ten Tips

FINALLY, HERE ARE MY Top Ten Tips to help start your own business:

1. Decide your level of investment
2. Source information on antiques venues, including local boot fairs, antique fairs, centres and auctions in specialist antique publications and online.
3. Plan to travel to different venues to source your items
4. Look beyond dirt and grime
5. Research necessary restoration skills and procedures
6. Research items for history and value

KNOW YOUR SUBJECT:

7. Look for a possible retail outlet and/or test your retail capabilities
8. Practice negotiating skills.
9. Read lots of books to expand your knowledge
10. Remember, there are always new lessons to be learned. Have an open mind.

Enjoy!